Energy Vortexes: Harnessing Power for UFO Summoning

Jessie Contreras

Published by Summon UFOs, 2024.

While every precaution has been taken in the preparation of this book, the publisher assumes no responsibility for errors or omissions, or for damages resulting from the use of the information contained herein.

ENERGY VORTEXES: HARNESSING POWER FOR UFO SUMMONING

First edition. September 13, 2024.

Copyright © 2024 Jessie Contreras.

ISBN: 979-8224463817

Written by Jessie Contreras.

Table of Contents

"To all aspiring UFO summoners—may your curiosity be boundless and your hearts be open. This book is dedicated to your fearless pursuit of the unknown and your desire to bridge the gap between worlds. Trust in your journey, embrace the mysteries, and may your efforts lead you to extraordinary encounters among the stars. Keep reaching for the cosmos!"

Chapter 1: The Concept of Energy Vortexes

1.1 Understanding Energy Vortexes in Nature

Energy vortexes are fascinating phenomena that can be described as swirling centers of energy, where the natural forces of the Earth seem to converge and intensify. When I first experienced an energy vortex, it felt like stepping into a different realm—like I was enveloped by an invisible force that both calmed and invigorated me. These vortexes can manifest as geographical features, where the land seems to hum with a unique vibrational frequency. Characteristics of energy vortexes often include heightened sensations, increased intuition, and unusual occurrences that can attract individuals seeking spiritual enlightenment or even more physical experiences, such as sightings of unexplained aerial phenomena.

Several locations around the globe are considered hotspots of energetic activity. One of the most famous examples is Sedona, Arizona, where the striking red rock formations are said to house powerful vortexes that draw visitors from far and wide. Many people report feelings of euphoria or deep introspection while hiking through this spectacular landscape. Another significant site is Mount Shasta in California, recognized not only for its majestic beauty but also for its reputation as a spiritual vortex that has often been linked to UFO sightings. The energy here is palpable, and the stories shared by those who have visited can be both intriguing and profound. Additionally, the Ley Lines in England, ancient pathways connecting various sacred sites, offer countless tales of energy flow and mystical happenings that suggest the Earth itself is alive with forces we have yet to fully understand. Exploring these locations provides not only a sense of adventure but also a deeper connection to the universe, which some believe could enhance the ability to summon UFOs or perceive their presence more clearly.

To tap into the energy of these vortexes, it helps to find a quiet moment in nature, allowing oneself to be open and receptive to whatever comes your way. Whether you're hiking in Sedona or meditating at Mount Shasta, focus on the sensations around you. Observe any subtle shifts in your feelings or thoughts. Connecting with these energies may enhance not just your awareness but also your ability to interact with the unexplained phenomena surrounding us.

1.2 Historical Perspectives on Vortexes

Ancient cultures have long been fascinated by the phenomena we now refer to as vortexes. In places like the Andes, the Nazca Lines are believed to be energy conduits that interact with the Earth's magnetic field. The indigenous people of the area held these sites in sacred regard, seeing vortexes as portals to the spirit world. In ancient Egypt, the pyramids were designed with specific alignments that correspond to cosmic events, hinting at a deep understanding of energy flows and vortex-like structures. They believed that these sites were both celestial and terrestrial connections that could elevate one's spirit. The Greeks also pondered about vortexes through the teachings of philosophers like Aristotle, who described whirlwinds and eddies as ways to understand nature's invisible forces. Each of these societies imbued vortexes with spiritual significance, seeing them as powerful areas, alive and teeming with energy, often used for rituals and ceremonies.

Throughout history, a number of prominent figures have recorded their experiences and encounters with these energy objects. One significant example is the renowned inventor Nikola Tesla, who explored the potential of harnessing energy from vortexes. He spoke of the ability to tap into universal energy, suggesting that such forces could be found both in nature and in our technological inventions. Another interesting figure is Edgar Cayce, a psychic known for his ability to tap into healing energies. He often referred to specific geographical locations believed to be energy vortexes that facilitated healing and psychic experiences. Even the famous artist Wassily Kandinsky mentioned his fascination with the energy swirling around us, expressing this idea through his abstract works. These encounters and reflections from various historical figures show a common thread: a connection to the unseen forces around us that many still seek to explore today. Their accounts serve as inspiration for anyone interested in discovering the energy behind UFOs.

Understanding the historical context of vortexes enriches our journey in seeking out their presence today. Ancient practices of meditation, energy work, and geomancy can be invaluable tools for resonating with these forces. For those keen on summoning UFOs, learning to recognize these energy hotspots may enhance your abilities to connect with anomalies in the sky. Consider visiting ancient sites known for their energetic properties, such as Sedona in Arizona or the Giza Plateau in Egypt. Engage with the land and its history, and open your senses to the vibrational presence of vortexes. This approach not only deepens your understanding but can also amplify your potential to encounter extraordinary phenomena.

1.3 The Connection Between Vortexes and UFO Phenomena

Investigating the theories linking energy vortexes to UFO sightings opens up a fascinating world of possibilities. Many believe that these so-called energy vortexes, filled with swirling energy and heightened electromagnetic fields, create portals or gateways that could attract unidentified flying objects. I found this idea compelling as I dove deeper into the research. A vortex is often described as a natural whirlpool of energy, and enthusiasts argue that these sites resonate with frequencies that might interact with the extraterrestrial. During my own explorations, whether hiking through Sedona's mesmerizing rock formations or visiting the mystical landscapes of Mount Shasta, the energy felt overwhelmingly palpable. I began to wonder if these surroundings truly had a connection to the unexplained aerial phenomena commonly reported in these areas. The more I learned, the more it seemed that UFO sightings might not just be random events but rather influenced by the very nature around us.

Sharing anecdotal experiences from those who have encountered UFOs at known vortex sites reveals another layer to this connection. As I spoke to fellow seekers, their stories were both intriguing and eerie. One person recounted spending an evening at a famous vortex in Arizona, where the sky began to change color, displaying hues of purple and blue that felt unnatural. Suddenly, out of nowhere, a bright light appeared, hovered silently for a moment, and then shot away at incredible speed. The thrill and fear intermingled as they described the sensation of being watched. Another account talked about a group camping near a vortex in Northern California when they witnessed a series of flashing lights zigzagging across the sky. They were drawn outdoors by an inexplicable urge and felt an overwhelming sense of connection with the universe. Hearing these stories fueled my curiosity and made me question what lies beyond our understanding.

Collectively, these experiences led me to reflect on how we might summon these enigmatic crafts ourselves. The trick seems to lie in our intention and energy alignment with the universe. Finding a vortex and immersing oneself within its energy could be a starting point. Being open and receptive to the environment, practicing mindfulness and meditation, and even using crystals for enhanced vibration could elevate the experience. Engaging in rituals or simply spending time in nature while focusing on connectivity may just invite sightings. It's all about tuning into the subtle energies around us and creating the right mental and spiritual space for an interaction with the unknown.

Chapter 2: The Science Behind UFOs

2.1 Exploring the Physics of UFOs

Many enthusiasts speculate about the technology behind UFOs, drawing from physics principles to explain their remarkable capabilities. One of the most intriguing areas of discussion is the concept of anti-gravity. If UFOs harness anti-gravitational forces, they could effortlessly defy the weight that our own technology struggles against. This theory often touches upon quantum mechanics, suggesting that manipulating gravitational fields might allow for extraordinary evasive maneuvers and speeds that defy our current understanding of propulsion. Additionally, the idea of warp drives—similar to those theorized in science fiction—could imply that UFOs might bend space-time, enabling them to traverse vast distances almost instantaneously, similar to how we perceive a shortcut through dimensions. It's a thrilling notion that pushes us to consider possibilities beyond conventional aircraft.

Evaluating these principles alongside known laws of physics is captivating. While anti-gravity remains largely hypothetical, researchers have uncovered phenomena such as the Casimir effect, hinting at manipulation of vacuum energy, which could potentially lead to breakthroughs in gravity manipulation. Moreover, there's an interesting alignment with Einstein's theories, particularly how mass and energy cannot be created or destroyed—only transformed. This principle might offer a foundation for understanding how UFOs convert energies into the propulsion systems they utilize. Moreover, exploring ideas like superconductivity and magnetic levitation suggests that resonating frequencies could be utilized to create lift without traditional engines. While there's still much debate, the possibilities pique our imaginations and inspire continued research.

Engaging with the complexities of these theories can stimulate innovative thinking. To enhance the likelihood of UFO sightings, consider experimenting with meditation techniques that focus on amplifying energy vibrations. This practice may create a harmonized state that aligns with the theoretical frequencies of UFO technology, ultimately facilitating encounters or sightings. By broadening our understanding of physics alongside practical exploration, we take a step closer to bridging the gap between our world and the mysteries above.

2.2 The Role of Extraterrestrial Energy Sources

Hypothesizing about the types of energy sources utilized by UFOs is both fascinating and complex. Many of us wonder what fuels these mysterious crafts that seem to maneuver in ways we can hardly comprehend. Picture this: a craft that effortlessly glides and accelerates, defying the known laws of physics. Some theorists suggest that these UFOs might harness energy from sources we have yet to fully understand—perhaps tapping into zero-point energy, which is a theoretical energy field existing at the quantum level. This form of energy could provide an almost unlimited and clean power source, a concept that might sound like science fiction but is being actively researched in some scientific circles. Others speculate that these crafts may utilize technologies involving antimatter, which could produce immense energy from relatively tiny amounts of mass. Imagine being able to compress more energy than we can currently produce on Earth into a compact space, providing propulsion and enabling interstellar travel. This brings us to wonder what types of technology these entities possess and how they've mastered energy control that remains elusive to us.

Considering how these energy sources may connect to earthly practices reveals striking parallels. Some us have begun exploring alternative energy sources like solar or wind, but what if we could adapt techniques inspired by what we imagine UFOs might use? For instance, the concept of harnessing energy fields or utilizing vibrations to create power isn't as far-fetched as it seems. Some cultural practices, such as using ancient rituals or meditative states to bridge connections beyond our physical realm, align closely with receiving communications from higher energies, potentially guiding us towards tapping into extraterrestrial knowledge. As we delve deeper into these energy forms, we might explore ways to enhance our consciousness or align our vibrations to create an openness that could summon these UFOs. Engaging in sound healing or using specific frequencies could tune us into these energy channels, fostering a connection that draws in these crafts. This reflective practice of integrating ancient wisdom with modern scientific understanding is where magic lies; by opening ourselves up and cultivating a greater awareness, we can not only align ourselves with these extraordinary energy patterns but also become co-creators of our cosmic fate, inviting these mysteries from the skies into our reality.

To begin your own exploration in summoning UFOs, consider starting a practice that unites mindfulness with intention. Meditative sessions, focused on enhancing your energy and consciousness, can create a receptive state. Use sound tools like crystal bowls or tuning forks during meditation to elevate your vibrations. Keep your mind open to the possibility of an energetic interaction beyond this world. The more you align with and understand these potential energy realms, the closer you could become to experiencing a connection with the unknown.

2.3 Theories on UFO Propulsion Mechanisms

Delving into the fascinating topic of how unidentified flying objects, or UFOs, might achieve flight brings to light a range of intriguing theories. Various ideas have emerged, suggesting that these crafts could potentially harness advanced technological principles far beyond our current understanding. Some theorize that UFOs utilize magnetic fields to counteract gravity, allowing them to hover or move with incredible agility. This principle is often compared to magnetic levitation trains, which glide above tracks without touching them. Others speculate that UFOs could be making use of advanced ion propulsion, where charged particles are expelled at high speeds, creating thrust. This concept isn't just science fiction; it's inspired by real studies on how ions can be manipulated for propulsion in our own spacecraft. Another captivating theory involves warp drives and wormholes, suggesting that UFOs might bend space-time itself to achieve faster-than-light travel. Such an idea, while still theoretical, opens our minds to possibilities that challenge the very fabric of our understanding of physics.

The implications of these theories for aerospace technology are profound and invite a re-evaluation of what we deem possible. If UFOs indeed operate on principles like these, it encourages us to investigate and innovate within our own aerospace programs. For example, by understanding and potentially mimicking the propulsion methods suggested in these theories, we could pave the way for new modes of transportation that could revolutionize how we view travel on Earth and beyond. This research could lead to advancements in energy efficiency and speed that we currently can only dream of. It raises the question of how far our current technological limitations might be stretched and challenges engineers and scientists to think outside conventional frameworks. As we explore these ideas, we tiptoe closer to bridging the gap between our earthly technology and possibly one day unlocking the secrets held by these enigmatic crafts.

Anyone interested in summoning UFOs should not only focus on the physical aspects but also the deeper understanding of these propulsion theories, as this knowledge may enhance personal encounters or observations. Consider becoming well-versed in the core principles of magnetism and ion propulsion; it may lead you to a unique vantage point during attempts to connect with these interstellar visitors. Engaging with the concepts of space-time or exploring the existing technologies within our aerospace field may enhance one's awareness and readiness for an extraordinary experience. Remember, staying open to the mysteries of the cosmos, coupled with scientific curiosity, could potentially open the door to encounters that many only dream of.

Chapter 3: Personal Energy Fields and Their Importance

3.1 Understanding Your Own Energy Field

The human energy field is often described as a glowing light or an aura that surrounds each of us, extending outwards and interacting with the world around us. Personally, I've always felt this energy as a warm vibration that can vary in intensity and color depending on my emotional state and physical well-being. Scientifically, this field is believed to consist of several layers, including the physical body, the emotional layer, and even more subtle dimensions like the mental and spiritual layers. Each of these dimensions plays a critical role in how I perceive and interact with the universe, sculpting my sense of self and affecting the energy I project to others. There's an undeniable connection between our energetic states and the experiences we attract, including encounters with unidentified flying objects. When I'm in a serene, open state, I feel more attuned to the energies around me, creating a more conducive environment for attracting something extraordinary.

To truly understand my own energy field, I've learned that exercising self-awareness is essential. I take quiet moments, sometimes during meditation or deep reflection, to assess my energy state. During these moments, I pay close attention to how my body feels and the emotions that surface. It's fascinating to notice the shifts in energy as my thoughts wander from anxiety to calmness. I've discovered that when I hold negative feelings, it feels like a heavy weight around me, which seems to repel positive experiences, including the cosmic connections I seek. Conversely, when I'm centered and grounded, my energy feels expansive and inviting. Engaging in practices like grounding—where I visualize roots growing from my feet into the earth—helps me to reconnect and stabilize my energy field. This grounded energy creates a magnetic pull, enhancing my capacity to connect with higher realms and possibly summon UFOs.

Being conscious of my energy not only elevates my vibration, but also opens a channel to the unknown. A practical tip I often rely on is to regularly check in on my energy, especially before embarking on any attempts to connect with extraterrestrial phenomena. I do this by closing my eyes, taking deep breaths, and visualizing the energy around me. If I feel any heaviness or discord, I take the time to clear it—sometimes through cleansing breaths or simple affirmations. This practice ensures that when I reach out into the cosmos, I'm doing so from a balanced and vibrant state of being.

3.2 Techniques for Strengthening Personal Energy

Identifying practices that can enhance personal energy levels has transformed my experiences in ways I never anticipated. For those of us seeking to connect with higher realms or summon UFOs, it becomes essential to cultivate a vibrant personal energy. Simple techniques such as meditation, breathwork, and mindful movement can significantly elevate our energy. When I first embraced meditation, I discovered a profound stillness that filled my mind and body with light. Focusing on my breath, I learned to let go of anxiety and invite in the vibrant energy around me. This practice allows me to raise my vibration, making me more receptive to the energies of the universe and its inhabitants.

Grounding and charging rituals are two activities that have deeply enriched my journey. Grounding, for me, often involves connecting with nature, whether it's standing barefoot on grass, hugging a tree, or simply lying down under the open sky. This connection not only stabilizes my energy but also helps to dispel any negativity I might be holding onto. Charging rituals can be equally powerful; I find that engaging with crystals or even sunlight can recharge my energy. There are moments when I'll hold a crystal in my hand, visualizing it absorbing and amplifying the vibrant energies that surround me. It's a dance of energy that fills my being with an invigorated sense of purpose, leaving me feeling open and ready to reach out to the cosmos. These practices have expanded my awareness, allowing me to tune into higher frequencies and increase my ability to connect with potential UFO sightings.

Each practice, whether grounding or charging, serves to create a space where I can thrive energetically. I encourage experimenting with various techniques to see what resonates best with you. Try to incorporate moments of stillness and connection in your daily life, as they can create the right conditions for tapping into those otherworldly energies. The key is maintaining a consistent practice, which for me has become a sacred ritual. This commitment to enhancing my personal energy has not just helped me in connecting with the universe, but it has also sparked an inner glow that draws forth the extraordinary.

3.3 How Personal Vortexes Influence UFO Summoning

Connecting personal energy to the ability to create energy vortexes is a profound experience that transcends the physical realm. I've come to realize that our personal energy, which often fluctuates based on our emotions and thoughts, plays a crucial role in the formation of these vortexes. In my early explorations of UFO summoning, I discovered that the meditative practices I engaged in helped to hone my energy levels. As I focused my intentions, I could feel a palpable shift—a kind of magnetic quality that seemed to pulse from within me. This energy, when cultivated effectively, allows us to create an environment that is conducive to attracting otherworldly visitors. It's almost as if the alignment between our personal energy and the natural energies around us creates a pathway for these phenomena to emerge. When we align our thoughts, intentions, and emotional states, we can effectively amplify our energy and, in turn, enhance our ability to harness these powerful vortexes.

Through many personal experiences, I've found that energy cultivation significantly affects my success in summoning UFOs. There was a night when I decided to practice a specific breathing technique while under the stars. I visualized energy swirling around me and merging with the vast cosmos. As I sat in stillness and absorbed the ambient sounds of the night, I felt a surge of energy build inside me. It was exhilarating, as if the world around me became charged with possibilities. During that evening, a faint light flickered in the distance, which transformed into a brilliant object darting across the sky. This moment was profound; it confirmed my understanding that the energy I cultivated directly correlated with the presence I attracted. When I focus my thoughts purely on the intention of summoning, eliminating any distractions, I find that the universe responds in kind.

Chapter 4: Identifying Locations of Energy Vortexes

4.1 Natural and Man-Made Vortexes

Understanding the difference between natural formations and human-created vortexes opens a fascinating window into our universe. Natural vortexes often arise from the Earth's own forces. Think about the majestic whirlpools found in rivers or the swirling winds of a tornado. These formations occur naturally, shaped by environmental conditions that have existed for eons. In contrast, man-made vortexes are intentionally engineered by individuals, often for purposes that explore or harness the forces of nature. The construction of these vortexes, such as those seen in certain experimental energy projects or even in UFO research, demonstrates humanity's desire to engage with and replicate natural phenomena in innovative ways.

Traveling across various regions, I've encountered both natural and man-made vortexes that leave an indelible mark on one's consciousness. In Sedona, Arizona, for instance, the Red Rocks form a backdrop to some of the most renowned natural vortexes, attracting seekers eager for spiritual renewal and UFO sightings alike. People gather at the energy centers, hoping to feel the heightened vibrational energy that many claim to experience. On the other hand, in the less-beaten path of the Mohave Desert, I came across a curious human-made vortex project aiming to communicate with extraterrestrial life. It was an ambitious setup of reflective materials and lights designed to amplify signals into the sky. Walking among these structures was an otherworldly experience, imagining the potential for contact beyond our earthly plane.

Sharing stories of these experiences can only deepen the intrigue. At the site of the Great Serpent Mound in Ohio, a natural formation shaped by ancient peoples, you can almost hear the whispers of those who believed in its mystical properties. They aligned this natural vortex site with celestial events, tapping into the energy that might just open doors to the unknown. Meanwhile, near the sleepy town of Joshua Tree, California, there is a less traditional site—a collection of spiral rocks, meticulously arranged by enthusiasts who wanted to create a man-made vortex. I joined a group there one night, hoping to commune with any visitors from outside our planet. The contrast between the ancient and the modern echoed through the desert air, enriching my understanding of what draws people to these enigmatic spaces.

4.2 Using Maps and Tools to Locate Vortexes

Identifying energy vortex locations can feel like a thrilling adventure, a quest into the unknown that holds the promise of uncovering hidden mysteries. Tools and resources that help pinpoint these vortexes are becoming increasingly available, revealing multiple approaches you can take. For instance, many people rely on online maps, which are not just plain tools but are gathering communities and knowledge bases around vortexes. You can access specialized websites where enthusiasts share their findings, complete with coordinates and detailed descriptions of their experiences. These platforms often include personal narratives that illustrate how energy shifts in these areas have influenced encounters, making the data feel vibrant and enticing. Additionally, geographic information systems (GIS) can be valuable; these advanced tools allow users to visualize areas where ley lines converge, suggesting possible vortex locations. Integrating these resources into your explorations can craft a path toward discovery and connection.

Once you have these tools at your disposal, understanding how to utilize them is key. Familiarize yourself with the features of online maps. Zoom in on areas that interest you, and scrutinize the photographs shared by others — things like unusual formations or plant varieties might hint at an energy vortex. Pay attention to the feedback from others who have visited these spots; sometimes it pays to follow trails carved out by those who came before you. Consider downloading apps that track geomagnetic activity or even those that highlight natural energy locations. When planning a visit to a suspected vortex, it helps to visualize the area dynamics through satellite imagery. Arrive during different times of the day to see how the light plays with the landscape; some practitioners advocate visiting during twilight, believing it's the perfect time to summon energies.

Always remember that while technology can guide your journey, your intuition is your greatest asset. Stay tuned in to your surroundings, keeping an open mind to sensations and energies that may present themselves. Be patient and maintain a sense of curiosity. Every location has its own story, and sometimes the most profound experiences occur when least expected. When venturing out to locate these vortexes, bring along simple tools like a compass or pendulum to help you navigate and tune in to energy shifts. Keep a journal to document your encounters and feelings; patterns may emerge over time, leading you to understand and interprete the nexus between these coordinates and your experiences with the unexplained.

4.3 Personal Experiences at Notable Vortex Sites

Sharing my firsthand experiences at various vortex sites has been nothing short of transformative. One of the most memorable locations was Sedona, Arizona. The moment I arrived, an inexplicable energy enveloped me. Strange currents seemed to pull at my very being, and I could feel my senses heightening. As I stood atop one of the iconic red rocks, I closed my eyes and tuned into the environment around me. I could hear whispers of the wind that felt almost like a conversation. Some say that vortexes amplify spiritual and psychic abilities, and I sensed that the site was indeed inviting a deeper connection with the energies surrounding me. There were moments I thought I could even glimpse through the veil, as if other realms were brushing against our own. The excitement and serenity coexisted within me, creating a unique bridge between the physical and metaphysical world.

Encouraging others to seek their own encounters at similar vortex locations is important to me. Each person experiences energy differently, and your own journey can lead to profound insights and connections. Consider visiting places known for their energetic properties, like Mount Shasta or the numerous sites in Peru. When you arrive, take the time to ground yourself. Start by simply standing still, breathing deeply, and allowing the surroundings to wash over you. You might want to journal your feelings or take photographs, but don't forget to put your phone down occasionally. This is about the experience, not just capturing it. Embrace the natural rhythms and let your intuition guide you. Each vortex site carries its own unique vibration—tap into that, and you might just find a link to something greater. Remember, the more open you are to the experience, the more likely you are to connect with the unseen.

As you embark on your journeys to these energetic lands, remain curious and patient. Practice mindfulness and listen to the whispers of the universe. Many have reported unexpected sightings and UFOs, often after feeling a deep connection with their surroundings. Your openness and the energy you carry may be the key to unlocking new experiences. Preparing yourself through meditation, intention-setting, and grounding techniques can enhance your ability to receive messages or glimpses of the extraordinary.

Chapter 5: Preparing for Summoning

5.1 Setting Intentions for UFO Summoning

Clarity is essential when it comes to summoning UFOs. The universe responds to intentions like a mirror reflects your thoughts and desires. When I first began this journey, I quickly learned that vague or scattered intentions resulted in equally unclear experiences. I recall the time I simply wished to see a UFO. While this intention sent an energy out into the universe, it lacked the specificity that could engage the UFO energies effectively. It's vital to approach this practice with a clear, focused mindset. The more precise your intention, the more effortlessly the universe can align with your desires. Instead of general desires, consider what you truly want to experience. Do you seek knowledge, contact, or perhaps an encounter for validation? Each of these focuses the energy in a different direction and can influence the nature of the experience.

Well-defined intentions can mold the type of interactions you have with UFO phenomena. For instance, instead of a simple request to see a spaceship, consider framing it in a more enriched context. You might state, I intend to establish a peaceful connection with extraterrestrial beings who wish to share their wisdom. This intention resonates deeply and aligns with higher vibrational energies, inviting open communication. Another example could be, I am ready to receive guidance from the universe about my place in cosmic existence. Such intentions not only open doors to sightings but also to profound insights. Reflecting on the energy you invoke can completely change the potential outcomes. Literally, the universe is waiting for your cue, so sending out a clear, vibrant message makes all the difference in the experiences you can potentially attract.

As you embark on your UFO summoning journey, remember to maintain an open heart and mind. When setting your intentions, engage in a meditative practice that enables you to attune to the energies around you. Picture your intention unfolding in your mind's eye and feel the excitement of that reality becoming true. Writing your intentions down can also strengthen your resolve and clarify your focus. Keeping your intentions visible—perhaps in a dedicated journal or on your altar—serves as a constant reminder of your commitment to the process. The clearer and stronger your intention, the more aligned your experience will be. Aim to set intentions that uplift your spirit and resonate deep within your core, and watch as the universe responds in ways you may never have imagined.

5.2 Creating a Sacred Space for Practice

Setting up a dedicated space for your UFO summoning practice is essential for focusing your energy and intention. Start by selecting a quiet corner in your home or outdoors where you feel comfortable and undisturbed. This space should resonate with you, a place where you can truly connect with your thoughts and the universe. The first step in creating this sacred environment is to declutter. Remove anything that does not serve your purpose or distracts you. A clean space allows for clearer energy flow and reduces mental noise.

Once you have a clean slate, it's time to enhance the energy of your space through decoration. Choose items that inspire you and evoke a sense of peace, wonder, or curiosity about the cosmos. Crystals, such as clear quartz or amethyst, can amplify your intentions. Plants can also add a vibrant, organic energy, so consider having a small potted plant or even some fresh flowers. Personal touches, like a piece of art that reflects your interest in UFOs or star maps, can help set the mood. Soft, ambient lighting—like candles or strings of fairy lights—will create a warm atmosphere, making it inviting and comfortable for your practice sessions. Remember, this space is a reflection of your inner world, so fill it with items that resonate with your goals and aspirations.

As you cultivate this dedicated space, take the time to regularly cleanse it energetically. You can do this through methods like burning sage or using sound bowls to shift any stagnant energy. Keeping your area energetically vibrant will not only enhance your practice but also strengthen your connection to the experiences you seek. The more you honor this space, the more it will honor your intent, creating an environment ripe for summoning UFOs and engaging with the mysteries of the universe.

5.3 Tools and Materials for Effective Summoning

Many people underestimate the impact that the right tools and materials can have on the process of summoning. Over the years, I've learned that having the right items not only amplifies the energy around you but also helps to focus your intention. At the core of successful summoning lies a selection of essential materials—like crystals, incense, and sound tools—that when combined, can create a powerful atmosphere conducive to contact. Crystals such as Moldavite or Amethyst are particularly potent; they are known to enhance spiritual energy. Similarly, natural elements like herbs, which can be burned or placed around your space, help in establishing a connection with the higher realms. A simple yet effective item is a comfortable chair or cushion, setting the stage for a focused mindset during the summoning process. All these elements work together to boost the vibrational energy needed for effective communication with extraterrestrial entities.

Each tool plays a distinct role in your summoning practice. Crystals act as amplifiers for energies, providing a conduit through which you can channel your intentions. When I use Moldavite, I often feel a sense of heightened awareness, as though my senses are finely tuned to receive signals. Burning scented herbs or incense, like sage or sandalwood, creates a cleansing environment, which clears out negative energies that might interfere with your connection. The act of creating ambient sounds, perhaps with singing bowls or gentle music, can heighten your state of relaxation and enable a deeper meditative state. This music holds an ancient resonance that harmonizes with the frequencies we are trying to align with. Each of these tools doesn't just serve a singular purpose; they interact and complement one another, weaving a tapestry of energy that envelops and supports your summoning efforts.

As you gather your materials, remember that intention is the most crucial aspect of summoning. Regardless of how impressive your collection might be, without a focused mindset, it may prove less effective. A practical tip I often share is to dedicate time to consciously infuse your tools with your intention before each session. Hold each crystal, light the incense, or play your music while concentrating on your goal and visualizing the energy you want to attract. This practice not only reinforces your intent but can also create a unique energetic signature, making each session more personalized and powerful.

Chapter 6: Meditation and Visualization Techniques

6.1 Guided Meditations for UFO Connection

In my journey to connect with the energies of UFOs, I discovered the power of guided meditations designed specifically for this purpose. These meditations are not just about sitting in silence; they are structured pathways that help to open our minds and hearts to the unknown. As I settled into a comfortable position, I began to focus on my breath, allowing the rhythmic flow to ground me. Guided meditations often incorporate visualization techniques that evoke vivid imagery of starry skies and cosmic spaces. I imagined myself floating in the vastness of the universe, surrounded by twinkling lights that shifted and danced like living beings. By engaging all my senses in this imaginative space, I felt a deeper connection to the energies that might be watching over us, inviting them into my awareness. Each session was unique, filled with a mix of anticipation and serenity. I discovered that inviting these extraterrestrial energies into my meditation created an atmosphere of tranquility and openness, allowing for a profound exchange beyond the physical realm.

The significance of deep focus during these sessions cannot be overstated. It is fundamentally about quieting the mind to create a sacred space within ourselves. When I approached these meditations, I realized that distractions from the outside world could interfere with my ability to connect. Therefore, I learned to set the environment carefully, ensuring it was free from interruptions. I turned off my phone, dimmed the lights, and sometimes even lit candles to enhance the atmosphere. Deep focus allows the mind to enter a state of receptivity, which is crucial for this type of spiritual exploration. When I dedicated my energy to concentrating solely on the visualizations and intentions, I often sensed an energetic shift around me. Whether it was a tingling sensation or a feeling of warmth, these signs reinforced my belief that I was connecting with something greater. By cultivating this state of focus, I could allow the UFO energies to share their messages and establish a deeper relationship with that cosmic presence.

For those seeking to embark on their own journey of UFO connection, consider creating a ritual around your practice. Whether it's specific crystals, calming sounds, or fragrant incense, these can help enhance your meditative experience. Personalizing the meditation space makes it a sanctuary dedicated to these explorations. It's essential to approach each session with an open mind and a sense of curiosity. Trusting the process and allowing yourself to be a channel for communication can lead to unexpected insights and experiences.

6.2 Visualization Exercises to Amplify Energy

Visualization techniques can be incredibly powerful in enhancing the summoning process, particularly when it comes to attracting UFOs. When I first started exploring this avenue, I realized that my imagination was a tool I could hone to direct my energy. It was essential to create vivid mental images that resonated with the feelings I wanted to experience during my summonings. I discovered that by visualizing the actual encounter—seeing the sleek, extraterrestrial craft hovering in the night sky—I could amplify my intentions and align my energy with those elusive visitors. The more detailed and immersive my visualization became, the stronger my connection felt. I would imagine the colors of the craft, the sound of its engines, and even the warmth of the light it emitted. Each session helped deepen my focus, making it easier to draw in the energy of potential encounters.

Guided imagery can serve as a wonderful tool to enhance this process further. Whenever I found myself struggling to maintain focus or feeling disconnected, I would use guided imagery to help channel my energy toward those desired outcomes. This technique involved creating a serene mental space where I could relax and open my mind to the possibilities. I would picture myself in a peaceful field, lying back on the soft grass while gazing up at the stars. With every inhale, I would visualize positive energy flowing into my body, and with every exhale, I would imagine releasing any doubts or fears I held. As I settled into this rhythmic breathing, I repeated affirmations that reinforced my intentions, such as, I am open to the wonders of the universe, and I attract positive energy that aligns with my dreams. Over time, I noticed that these visualizations made my summonings feel more potent and intentional.

Incorporating visualization exercises into your routine doesn't require a lot of time. Setting aside just a few minutes each day for these practices can significantly elevate your energy levels and enhance your connection with the unknown. You may want to keep a journal documenting your experiences, noting any changes or encounters that arise after your visualization sessions. This practice not only keeps track of your growth but also reinforces your commitment to the process. Remember, clarity in your visualizations directly correlates to how effectively you can summon the energy you desire.

6.3 Documenting Your Experiences Post-Meditation

Keeping a meditation journal has become one of my most cherished practices. It's amazing how a simple act of writing can deepen the understanding of my meditation experiences. Each entry serves as a snapshot of my thoughts, feelings, and insights, allowing me to capture the subtle shifts that occur during those tranquil moments. The act of recording not only reinforces my commitment to meditating but also enriches my practice. I encourage you to reflect deeply on your meditative sessions and write about it afterward. Describe the sensations, the visions, or the emotions that might arise. Over time, you'll start to notice patterns, specific triggers, or themes that repeat, which can help in your future summoning efforts. By keeping a detailed journal, you create a roadmap of your personal journey into the realm of UFO summoning, giving you a resource to look back on whenever you need a boost of confidence or clarity.

The value of reflection cannot be overstated. When I take the time to look back through my journal, I often find nuggets of wisdom that I didn't appreciate in the moment. Reflection allows me to distill my experiences—what worked, what didn't, and how I felt during each session. I can pinpoint moments of clarity or confusion, moments when I felt a strong connection to the universe, and times when distraction held me captive. This process of reflecting enhances my ability to summon UFOs, as I'm more aware of my emotional and energetic states. For anyone wishing to connect with UFOs, understanding these subtle nuances is crucial. Each reflection reminds me that my journey is unique, and every session contributes to my overall growth.

Finally, think of your meditation journal as a living document of your experiences. It's not just about noting what happens during meditation; it's about charting your emotional landscape and spiritual growth. Whenever you sit down to meditate, do so with the intention of later documenting your experience. After each session, take a moment to jot down everything that comes to mind without censoring yourself. This raw data can be instrumental in your UFO summoning practices down the line. The more you can identify what brings you closer to those elusive experiences, the more effective your summoning will become. Begin today, and let your journal be the guide that leads you toward the extraordinary.

Chapter 7: Rituals and Practices for Manifestation

7.1 Crafting Your Own Summoning Ritual

Designing a personalized summoning ritual can be one of the most fulfilling experiences for anyone keen on connecting with UFOs. The beauty of such a ritual is that it can reflect your unique energies, beliefs, and intentions. The first step is to define what you hope to accomplish. Are you looking for communication, guidance, or simply an experience? Once you have a clear intention, gather elements that resonate with you. These could be specific objects like crystals, candles, or symbols that have personal significance. Incorporate colors that align with your energy and intent, as colors can amplify your focus. Setting the space is equally vital; create an environment that feels safe and welcoming, allowing your energy to flow freely. Natural settings, sacred spaces at home, or even a quiet corner where you won't be disturbed can work wonders. Remember, your intention will guide the energy you summon.

Encouraging creativity in your ritual allows for deep personal engagement. Trust your intuition throughout the process; it's your inner voice that will guide you best. Consider the sounds that might enhance your ritual—maybe a specific type of music or nature sounds that draw you in. You could also create or choose affirmations that resonate with your goals. Utilizing meditation or visualization techniques can help solidify your intentions, enhancing your psychic receptiveness. Each element you include should feel right to you, even if it seems unconventional. Perhaps you feel drawn to use an ancient symbol or unique scent that reminds you of a powerful vision. Embrace that instinctive drive. The more you involve your individuality in the process, the stronger the connection may become. A powerful ritual isn't about strict adherence to established norms; it thrives on the unique blend of purpose and personal creativity.

As you embark on this journey, I've found that preparing a grounded mindset is just as essential as the components of the ritual itself. Take a moment to clear your mind and center your energy before invoking powers. This not only enhances your energy but also opens your heart. After the summoning, take time to document your feelings and any experiences you have. Keeping a journal about these practices can reveal patterns and insights over time, enhancing your next rituals. Remember, persistence and openness to learning are keys to nurturing these connections in your journey. A practical tip: never underestimate the power of personal experience; every ritual will teach you something new, so let your journey unfold naturally and joyfully.

7.2 Utilizing Crystals and Their Energies

Each crystal carries its own unique vibrations and energies that can be incredibly beneficial when it comes to summoning. For instance, clear quartz is well-known for its amplification properties; it can boost the energies of other crystals, making it an essential tool for those wanting to increase their potential for contact. Amethyst, with its higher vibrational frequency, is excellent for spiritual protection and opening up the third eye, allowing us to enhance our intuition. I have found that working with labradorite can help create a strong barrier against negative energies, which is particularly useful during summoning rituals. Blue lace agate, often recommended for its calming properties, aids in effective communication, making it easier to connect with otherworldly beings. It's all about selecting the right crystals based on the specific energies you aim to attract or the assistance you require on your journey into the unknown.

Incorporating crystals into your rituals is a deeply personal and intuitive process. When preparing for a summoning session, I usually create a dedicated sacred space where I place my crystals strategically. By arranging them in a circle or placing them around my central focus point, I invite the energies of each stone to interact and support the summoning. Before each session, I like to cleanse my crystals—whether through sound, smoke, or moonlight—ensuring they are charged and ready to work. Additionally, holding a crystal in your hand while visualizing your intention can significantly enhance the experience. I often chant or meditate with the crystals, allowing their energies to align with mine, creating a powerful synergy that increases my focus and intention. You may also want to consider keeping a crystal grid to maintain a continuous flow of energy, promoting a sacred space for communication when you're not actively engaging in rituals.

Always remember, the process of working with crystals requires patience and tuning into your own energies. It's essential to trust your intuition when selecting and using crystals during your sessions. One practical tip is to keep a journal of your experiences, noting the type of crystals used and the outcomes of your rituals. Over time, you will begin to recognize patterns or energies that resonate with you personally. This practice not only deepens your understanding but can also enhance your ability to summon effectively. Embracing the energy of the crystals around you may just open up new dimensions of your experience.

7.3 The Role of Sound and Music in Vortex Energy

Sound has a remarkable ability to influence our environment and the energies around us. In the context of summoning UFOs, specific sounds can create vibrations that resonate with the energies of the universe. When I first began my journey into summoning, I experimented with different tones and frequencies, discovering that certain sounds seemed to draw energy toward me. The universe responds to resonance, and creating the right sonic environment can enhance the calling process. Certain natural sounds, like the rustling of leaves or the gentle flow of water, have an innate connection with our planet's energy grids. By incorporating these elements into a ritual, you might find yourself better aligned with the energy needed to open a vortex for UFOs to arrive.

For those looking to engage in a summoning ritual, I recommend using specific music and sounds that elevate your frequency and intention. Ambient music with sustained notes can help you enter a meditative state, creating a conducive atmosphere for summoning. Try using Tibetan singing bowls or crystal bowls, which produce rich, resonant sounds that can aid in raising your vibration. Additionally, tracks with binaural beats can help synchronize your brainwaves to the frequencies associated with higher states of consciousness. Another powerful option is to create a soundscape combining nature sounds with soft instrumental music, allowing you to immerse yourself completely in the experience. Remember, the energy you put into your ritual is just as important as the sounds you choose, so ensure you're in a calm and focused state.

As you prepare for your summoning practice, consider the time of day and the surrounding environment. Twilight can be an ideal backdrop as the energies of the day transition into night. Playing sounds or music that resonate with you in this setting can augment your efforts. Experiment with different combinations to find what feels right for you. Ultimately, pay attention to how each sound and piece of music affects your energy, and use those insights to refine your rituals further. This interaction between sound and energy is not just an abstract concept; it is a tangible process through which you can deepen your connection with the cosmic forces at play.

Chapter 8: Working with Spirit Guides and Beings

8.1 Identifying Your Spirit Guides

Recognizing your personal spirit guides can be an enlightening journey. These guides often connect with us in ways that may seem subtle at first. I remember my first encounter vividly; I was in a quiet park, meditating under a large oak tree when I felt a gentle presence beside me. It wasn't just the serene environment that inspired this feeling; it was almost as if a warmth enveloped me, prompting me to look beyond the physical realm. Many people experience these guides during meditation or in moments of deep introspection, where the distractions of the world fade away. Pay attention to your instincts and feelings during these moments, as spirit guides often communicate through subtle nudges, emotional responses, or even vivid dreams. When you recognize these signs, you deepen your connection to the support that awaits you.

Your spirit guides are here to assist you on your journey, particularly as you delve into your practice of summoning UFOs. They provide insights, offer protection, and help clarify your intentions. For instance, I often ask my guides for clarity before attempting to make contact with extraterrestrial life. I find it helpful to create a sacred space where I feel safe and protected, and then invite my guides to join me. It's in these moments that I hear their whispers of encouragement or wisdom, guiding me to focus on specific stars or locations in the sky. The more you engage with your guides, the more you'll understand how they can enhance your experiences, providing a sense of comfort and direction.

To strengthen your connection with your spirit guides, practice journaling after your meditations or UFO summoning sessions. Write down any feelings, thoughts, or messages you receive. These notes can reveal patterns or insights over time, helping you recognize your guides more clearly. Remember, your relationship with them is a partnership, and they are eager to assist you. As you nurture this bond, your ability to communicate with the cosmos will flourish.

8.2 Communicating with Extraterrestrial Beings

Opening channels for communication with extraterrestrials is an exciting venture that ignites the imagination. It begins with the understanding that we are all part of a vast universe filled with diverse forms of life. To connect with these beings, one must first cultivate a mindset of openness and curiosity. Meditative practices can be instrumental in this regard. When I first attempted to communicate with UFOs, I found that quieting my mind and focusing on my intentions allowed me to create a space where communication could flow. Using techniques like visualization, you can imagine a bright light surrounding you, inviting extraterrestrial beings to join the experience. Nature can be a powerful ally in this journey. I recommend taking your sessions outdoors under a clear sky, where the energy feels more vibrant, and connecting with the stars can make the experience feel more resonant.

As you move forward, clarity becomes essential in these communications. It's crucial to express your thoughts and intentions clearly and confidently. I discovered that writing down specific questions or messages before a session helped me remain focused. Rather than feeling scattered or overwhelmed, having tangible points to refer back to kept me grounded in the experience. When I communicated, I tried to speak as if I were addressing an old friend—inviting familiarity and warmth into the interaction. You might also want to practice grounding exercises to settle any nervous energy. Standing barefoot on the earth, breathing deeply, and envisioning your energy merging with the ground can create a solid foundation for respectful and meaningful communication. Trust your intuition throughout the process; if you feel a connection, lean into it, as our intuitive senses can often perceive the subtle shifts when the energy around us changes.

As you explore this fascinating journey, remember that honing your skills takes patience and practice. Every attempt to communicate brings you closer to understanding the signals and messages you may receive. Setting a specific time for these sessions may also create a routine that aids the connection. A practical tip is to keep a journal documenting your experiences, feelings, and the interactions you have. Recording your journey not only helps you notice patterns but also invites clarity into your purpose as you reach out to the cosmos and its inhabitants.

8.3 Integrating Guidance into Your Summoning Practice

Incorporating insights from guides into your rituals can significantly enhance your summoning practice. When I first began exploring the world of UFO summoning, I quickly realized that my connection with these otherworldly beings was not solely about my intentions; it was about being open to the messages and guidance that came from other dimensions. I found that keeping a journal of my experiences helped capture the subtle nudges and signs that emerged during rituals. As I would prepare for a session, I would meditate specifically on what I hoped to learn or receive from my guides. This focused intention allowed me to better recognize the nuances in the energy around me, leading to richer connections during my summoning practices. Integrating recommendations from trusted sources or intuitive insights from meditative states can transform a standard ritual into a deeply personal experience, enlightening both your path and your purpose at that moment.

Flexibility and responsiveness in summoning cannot be overstated. The universe is dynamic, and the energies we seek to connect with can shift instantaneously. During one of my sessions, I had prepared a very specific meditation, expecting clear signs in the form of lights flickering or auditory confirmations. Instead, I felt an unexpected urge to change my approach halfway through. Listening to this instinct, I started to reframe my meditation, emphasizing gratitude and openness rather than expectation. It was in that moment of adaptability that I began experiencing a surge of energy, and suddenly, I witnessed a brilliant flash of light overhead. It became a profound reminder that while intention is crucial, the ability to adjust and respond to the energy around us is equally essential. Be willing to flow with the guidance you receive, whether through intuition, signs, or even the air around you, because sometimes, the universe has surprises that exceed our expectations.

In practice, always remember that your connection with guides is an ongoing journey. Each ritual you conduct serves as a stepping stone towards deeper understanding. The more you engage with your guides and summon with sincerity, the more you may unravel the potential within your practice. Consider attending local groups focusing on UFO summoning and sharing experiences or participating in online forums. Discussing your insights with others can expand your perspective and cultivate greater clarity in your own practices. Keeping an open mind and heart, recognizing the wisdom that comes from guidance, and adapting your approach based on what resonates with you can significantly enrich your summoning experiences. Remain curious, and you may just find that the universe has a wealth of insights waiting for you to discover.

Chapter 9: Harnessing Natural Elements

9.1 Using Earth, Air, Fire, and Water in Practices

Understanding the role of the four natural elements—Earth, Air, Fire, and Water—in energy work is essential for anyone looking to connect with the universe beyond our planet. Each element carries its own unique energy and qualities that can enhance our intention when summoning UFOs. Earth signifies stability and grounding, anchoring our energy and offering a solid foundation for our practices. It reminds us to stay connected to our physical surroundings, ensuring that we remain balanced during our explorations. Air, on the other hand, embodies communication and freedom. It allows our intentions to rise and travel, much like how thoughts and signals move through the airwaves. Fire signifies transformation and passion; it can ignite our desire to connect with extraterrestrial beings and fuel our rituals with vibrant energy. Lastly, Water represents intuition and emotion, facilitating a deeper connection to the unseen realms and helping us to tap into the collective consciousness that surrounds us.

Incorporating these elements into your summoning practices can be a transformative experience. Begin by creating a sacred space where you feel comfortable and at ease. As you prepare, think about the qualities of each element and how they resonate with your intention. You might choose to light candles to represent fire, place stones or crystals to symbolize earth, use an essential oil or incense to invoke air, and have a bowl of water nearby to embody its essence. Focus on your breath, allowing the air element to fill you with clarity and purpose. As you invoke the energies, visualize them swirling around you, merging with your intention. When summoning, speak your desires and thoughts clearly, allowing the air to carry your voice to the cosmos. Feel the grounding weight of the earth beneath you, the passionate fire within you, and the flowing water that connects you to all life. This holistic approach will enrich your summoning practice, creating a profound resonance that can attract the attention of UFOs.

Remember, the act of summoning is not just about asking; it's about creating a shared dialogue with the universe. Cultivating a respectful relationship with these elements will enhance your experience. As you build your practice, pay attention to how each element influences your feelings and responses. Developing this sensitivity will make your ability to summon increasingly powerful. Each session can deepen your understanding of how these natural forces align with your intentions. Embrace this journey with openness and curiosity, and you may find that the elements not only aid in your summoning efforts but also reveal insights about your own path forward.

9.2 Seasonal Changes and Their Impact on Energy

The seasons hold a profound influence over not just nature, but also the energy that resonates around us and within ourselves. Each season brings a unique energy signature, shaping our experiences and the way we connect with the universe. Spring bursts forth with vibrant energy, awakening life from its winter slumber. This season encourages us to harness the freshness and renewal of new beginnings, making it an ideal time for rituals focused on growth and manifestation. I remember standing in a field surrounded by blooming flowers, feeling a wave of inspiration wash over me. It felt like every petal whispered secrets from beyond, urging me to dream bigger and reach higher. In contrast, summer brings warmth and abundance, urging us to celebrate and share. This is the season to gather, to commune with others, and to celebrate what you have manifested. The long days and bright nights can heighten our ability to connect with extraterrestrial energies, feeling vibrant and alive as the sun strengthens its hold on the world.

As we transition into autumn, a different energy envelops us. The days become shorter, signaling a time of reflection and release. During this season, it's beneficial to practice rituals that honor what we have accomplished while letting go of what no longer serves us. I often find myself outside, collecting fallen leaves and envisioning the energy of my intentions being carried into the wind, letting nature do the work of dispersing them into the universe. Winter, with its quieter, introspective energy, offers a sacred space for deep contemplation and connection with the cosmos. The stillness allows us to tune into the frequencies of the universe and is an excellent time to focus on summoning practices. By aligning my meditative practices with these winter energies, I feel an increased clarity and connection with the galactic realms.

Embracing seasonal rituals can deepen our experience of these energetic shifts. For instance, during spring, creating a garden altar with seeds and intentions can set a powerful tone for the season. Summer is perfect for night sky gatherings, where you might share stories under the stars, amplifying your collective energy. As autumn approaches, a simple ritual of writing down what you want to release and burying it in the earth can help you connect with the cycles of life and death. In the winter months, find a quiet space to meditate, focusing on the patterns of the stars and your connection to them. Trust that your energy is being heard, and remember that each season offers its own gifts in our journey of summoning. Knowing how to align your energy with the cycles of nature can enhance your ability to draw in experiences from beyond—opening doors to the extraordinary.

9.3 Eco-Friendly Practices for Vortex Work

Engaging with energy vortexes while remaining eco-friendly might seem like a challenging balance, but it can be quite fulfilling. Whenever I prepare for my vortex practices, I make a conscious decision to respect the environment. It's essential to choose locations that are not only energetically promising but also ecologically preserved. Seeking out natural landscapes that haven't been tampered with, like untouched forests or serene lakes, enhances the experience while protecting our planet. I also pay attention to my footprint. I use biodegradable materials for any offerings, and I ensure that nothing I bring into nature contributes to litter or damaging waste. Simple acts, like cleaning up any trash I might find along my journey, create a ripple effect of positive energy and sustainability.

For those of you aspiring to summon UFOs, infusing your practice with eco-conscious habits will enhance your connection not just to the cosmos, but also to the Earth itself. Start by cultivating your own energy garden at home. Planting herbs, flowers, or even trees creates a nurturing space filled with positive vibrations. The air quality improves, and you'll find that spending time among greenery elevates your emotional and spiritual state. When engaging in group summoning sessions, encourage participants to bring reusable materials, such as water bottles and eco-friendly snacks. Not only does this minimize waste, but it also initiates conversations about the significance of environmental stewardship. Always remember, the connections we foster with extraterrestrial beings may be deeply linked to how we treat our own world.

As you delve into these practices, consider carrying a small journal to note your experiences and reflections. This will help you maintain a deeper connection with both the energies you're seeking and the environment that supports them. With each entry, you contribute to the awareness of sustainable practices, creating an innovative community of UFO summoners who care for our planet while reaching for the stars.

Chapter 10: Documenting Experiences and Results

10.1 Keeping a UFO Summoning Journal

Journaling has always been a powerful tool for personal growth, and when it comes to the intriguing world of UFO summoning, it becomes even more vital. Keeping a UFO summoning journal allows us to track our experiences, thoughts, and emotions related to our attempts. Each entry captures a snapshot of our journey, serving not just as a record but also as a catalyst for reflection. As I look back on my own experiences, I realize that my journal has helped clarify my intentions, identify patterns, and even chart progress in ways I would never have imagined. The act of writing things down can reveal insights that might otherwise remain hidden, making it essential for anyone wishing to deepen their understanding and practice in this area.

When starting your UFO summoning journal, think about what you'd like to document. Include details such as dates, times, and locations of each summoning attempt, as well as the weather conditions and any notable celestial events. This information can later help connect the dots between different experiences. Additionally, jot down your thoughts before and after each session. What were your feelings? Did you approach the session with excitement, skepticism, or a mixture of both? Record any sensations or insights experienced during the summoning. Did you notice changes in your surroundings? Any unexplained visuals or sounds? These observations can be crucial in discerning patterns or shifts in energy linked to your summoning efforts. Journaling not only captures the tangible data but also chronicles your personal evolution—a true reflection of a journey that is equal parts science, mysticism, and self-discovery.

As you continue to fill your journal, consider including sketches or photographs of the sky above you during your sessions. Visual elements can bring your words to life and provide a fuller picture of the experiences you encounter. You might also want to note any relevant research or insights gained from books, documentaries, or communities that resonate with your journey. Over time, you'll find that your journal evolves alongside you, becoming a treasure trove of knowledge and inspiration. One practical tip is to set a specific time after each session to write in your journal. This will help create a ritualistic approach to your summoning practice, further engaging your mind and spirit in the endeavor. The more dedicated you are to this craft, the more insights and experiences you'll document—everything plays a part in your extraordinary journey toward contacting the unknown.

10.2 Analyzing Patterns and Frequencies

It's crucial to pay attention to the trends in your summoning experiences. Every time you attempt to reach out to UFOs, jot down the details. These notes might reveal subtle patterns that can significantly enhance your connection. For instance, you may notice certain times of the day or specific locations yielding more encounters. Perhaps it's on a clear night, or during a particular phase of the moon. By observing these factors, you'll start to identify what conditions seem to lead to more success. Tracking these trends can transform your approach, guiding you towards optimal conditions for summoning. Embracing these insights encourages a mindset of curiosity and discovery that can be thrilling in your quest. The more aware you become of these trends, the more informed and powerful your summoning attempts can be.

After recognizing and understanding these patterns, it's important to adapt your practices based on your observations. If you find that certain locations seem to attract UFOs more often, make those places a regular part of your summoning routine. Maybe you notice a correlation between your emotional state and the frequency of sightings. On nights when you feel calm and centered, you see more activity. This insight can direct you to incorporate relaxation techniques, such as meditation, into your preparation. Modifying your practices based on what you learn isn't just recommended; it can lead to extraordinary experiences. Remember, each failed attempt offers valuable data as much as a successful one does. Adaptation is key, so be flexible and open to changing tactics based on what your summoning experiences reveal.

By meticulously observing and recording your experiences and then making informed adjustments to your practices, you equip yourself with the tools to enhance your UFO summoning efforts. An effective way to stay organized is to maintain a journal dedicated solely to your summoning sessions. This will help build a narrative of your journey, allowing you to study your growth and development over time. As you collect more data, your ability to summon effectively will grow richer and more nuanced. Every detail counts, so keep your senses sharp and stay engaged with the process. Happy summoning!

10.3 Sharing Experiences with a Community

Sharing insights within a community focused on summoning UFOs has immense value. When people come together to discuss their experiences, ideas, and discoveries, it creates a rich tapestry of knowledge that no single person can achieve alone. I remember the first time I participated in a discussion group about UFO sightings. It was exhilarating to hear different perspectives, strategies, and even misconceptions that others had encountered. Each story offered a unique lens through which to view my pursuits, expanding my understanding and sparking new ideas. These shared moments not only educated but also fostered a sense of belonging. When you realize others are on a similar journey, it transforms the solitary act of skywatching into a collective adventure filled with camaraderie.

Platforms for community engagement are abundant, and exploring them can enhance your learning curve significantly. Social media groups dedicated to UFO enthusiasts offer a wealth of discussion and real-time advice. Additionally, local meetups provide opportunities to interact face-to-face, share stories, and even organize skywatching events together. I found that attending a few gatherings opened doors to friendships and collaborations that enriched my experience immensely. For those who prefer a more structured learning environment, online webinars and workshops focusing on UFO summoning techniques can be incredibly helpful. Explore forums where you can ask questions and share findings; participating actively in such spaces can help fine-tune your methods and expand your repertoire.

Joining or forming a UFO community, whether online or in-person, not only enhances your own experience but contributes to a larger body of knowledge. As you share your insights and learn from others, you may develop innovative techniques or theories. Engaging with fellow enthusiasts keeps the passion alive and creates a supportive network that encourages exploration. If you're looking to create connections, consider starting a blog or a video channel where you express your experiences, invite feedback, and promote discussions. Such platforms can inspire a wave of engagement and lead others to share their stories, enriching the entire community.

Chapter 11: Overcoming Doubts and Fears

11.1 Common Misconceptions About UFOs

Many people hold onto myths about UFOs that can really limit their openness to exploring the topic further. One of the biggest misconceptions is that sightings are purely a product of overactive imaginations or misidentification of ordinary objects. It's easy to dismiss a bright light in the sky as an airplane or a satellite rather than consider the possibility of something more extraordinary. This skepticism often grows from misunderstandings fueled by media portrayals, making it seem like anyone who believes in UFOs is simply a conspiracy theorist or someone lacking critical thinking.

Another widespread belief is that government entities have everything under control and that UFOs pose no real threat. This can lead people to think that if they don't see credible evidence from official sources, there's nothing to investigate. However, many first-hand accounts come from pilots and credible witnesses whose experiences challenge conventional explanations. By focusing too much on what we hear on the news or what the government chooses to release in terms of information, we can miss out on a wealth of knowledge and experience that is available through personal reports and research.

To clarify these misconceptions, it's essential to look at the broader perspective and understand that believing in UFOs doesn't mean following blind faith. It involves an open-minded pursuit of knowledge, supported by numerous credible encounters documented over the decades. Researchers and everyday people alike have provided substantial evidence pointing toward the reality of UFOs and unidentified aerial phenomena (UAP). Exploring various accounts, photographs, and even government disclosures can help us piece together a clearer picture. If you're curious about summoning UFOs and wish to engage with this phenomenon, remember to stay informed and critical—use your intuition but ground your beliefs in facts. A practical tip is to keep a journal of your observations and thoughts; this will help you track patterns and refine your approach to witnessing the unexplained.

11.2 Facing Fear: My Personal Journey

Fear has a strange way of gripping you, especially when it comes to something as unconventional as summoning UFOs. I remember my first experience vividly. I had spent countless nights reading about UFO sightings and the stories of those who claimed to have called upon them. The excitement was palpable, yet an undercurrent of dread coursed through me. What if something happened? What if I encountered something I couldn't explain? These thoughts dominated my mind, creating a barrier between me and the extraordinary possibilities that lay ahead.

One evening, I decided to face those fears head-on. I gathered my materials, including crystals, candles, and recorded messages to the universe. I set up my space meticulously, one part of me hoping it would conjure a feeling of safety. Yet, each sound—the rustling of leaves, the creaking of the nearby trees—felt amplified. It was an overwhelming cocktail of anticipation and trepidation. As I began my rituals, I took deep breaths, forcing myself to anchor down my fears. Slowly, I realized that my fear of the unknown was holding me back from experiencing something profound. I focused on my intent, pouring my energy into the act of summoning, and as I shifted my mindset, those fears began to dissipate. I learned that courage doesn't mean the absence of fear; it means moving forward regardless.

If you find yourself standing on the precipice of fear, remember that you're not alone. It's easy to let fear dictate our choices, particularly in the face of something as mysterious as UFO summoning. However, confronting those fears can open doors to remarkable experiences. Start small; perhaps try visualizing a safe encounter and gradually work up to the actual practice. Engage with your fears, ask them questions, and understand what lies beneath them. It becomes easier to move past those feelings when you acknowledge and embrace them. You have the power to rewrite your narrative and create a new story of exploration and discovery. So, when you feel that shiver of fear next time, let it be the fuel that propels you into the unknown rather than a chain that binds you.

For those looking to summon UFOs, try journaling your thoughts and feelings before and after your attempts. This can help track your progress and provide insights into your personal journey. By reflecting on your experiences, you will discover patterns and perhaps even learn how to navigate your emotions more effectively in the process.

11.3 Building Faith and Trust in Your Practice

Strengthening faith in the summoning process is essential for anyone eager to connect with UFOs. It begins with a deep understanding of your intentions and the clarity of your purpose. Each time I prepare for a session, I remind myself that the universe operates on frequencies, and by tuning into the right one, I can enhance my experience. Visualizing the connection can significantly amplify faith. Picture the UFO arriving, feel the excitement of contact, and envision the beings that may come. This mental imagery builds a strong foundation of belief. Over time, I found that incorporating rituals, such as meditative breathing and energy alignment practices, fosters a deeper trust in this process. As I align my thoughts and energies, I feel more connected, and this strengthens my faith in what I am trying to achieve.

Sharing affirmations and celebrating successes can help reinforce trust in your practice. After each session, I take time to reflect on even the smallest achievements. Perhaps I saw a light flicker in the distance, or I felt a subtle shift in the atmosphere. By writing these experiences down and expressing gratitude, I create a positive feedback loop that strengthens my resolve. I also find it beneficial to share these experiences with a community of like-minded individuals. Hearing their stories and affirmations can be incredibly uplifting. It's a reminder that we are all on a journey together, and each little success adds to the collective energy of belief. Encouragement flows both ways, and when you witness the triumphs of others, it fosters an environment where trust can flourish.

A practical tip to nurture faith and trust is to establish a dedicated space for your summoning practice. This can be as simple as a corner of your room where you feel most at peace. Fill it with items that resonate with your purpose, perhaps crystals or photographs of celestial objects. Each time you enter this space, you cultivate an atmosphere of expectation and openness. The energy you invest will return to you, deepening your belief and building your trust in the incredible experiences that await you.

Chapter 12: The Role of Group Summoning

12.1 Benefits of Summoning with a Collective

When we gather together to summon, something remarkable happens. The energy in the room shifts, amplifying the intentions of everyone present. I've experienced this firsthand; in those moments of collective focus, it feels as though we become a single entity united by a common goal. The heightened energy is palpable, as if we are drawing on an invisible force that enhances our individual efforts. I remember one particular night when a small group of us came together in a park, armed with nothing but our open minds and a determination to reach beyond the stars. As we formed a circle, our shared intent—the desire to connect with UFOs—seemed to vibrate in the air around us. It was electric. Each person's enthusiasm seemed to feed into the collective, creating an energetic feedback loop. This amplification doesn't just heighten the chances of success; it transforms the experience into something deeply fulfilling and communal.

The emotional and psychological benefits of practicing together are equally profound. Sharing such a personal and often vulnerable experience creates bonds that might not develop in more conventional settings. In my own journey, I've found that participating in group summoning sessions fosters a sense of belonging and camaraderie. There's an unspoken understanding among us, an acknowledgment that we are all seekers on the same path. This shared quest alleviates feelings of isolation that can sometimes come with these interests; it's reassuring to know that others are as curious and driven as I am. When we succeed in connecting with something beyond our realm together, the joy is multiplied, and the defeat, should it occur, feels lighter to bear. Each session is a healing experience, allowing us to express our hopes and fears in a supportive environment.

For anyone interested in summoning UFOs, consider the incredible power of summoning as a group. Not only can the collective energy enhance your chances of success, but the bonds formed during these sessions can transform your journey into one of laughter, support, and communal discovery. Finding a group to join or even starting one can be life-changing. Keep your heart open, invite others who share your passion, and prepare to be amazed by what you can achieve together.

12.2 Organizing Group Gathering Events

Setting up effective group summoning events requires not just planning but also a deep understanding of what creates a successful collective experience. First, considering the location is crucial; it should be a space that's both accessible and allows for some isolation from urban distractions. A quiet park, a spacious backyard, or even a remote campsite can serve as excellent venues. When I first organized such an event, I discovered the importance of timing as well. Evening gatherings seem to hold a certain magic, with the night sky above creating an immersive atmosphere conducive to collective focus. Make sure to choose a night when the moon isn't too bright to allow for optimal visibility of the stars and any possible UFOs. It's also beneficial to communicate clearly with participants beforehand about what to expect, the attire they should wear, and what items to bring, like blankets, snacks, or any personal items for spiritual or meditative practices.

Creating a comfortable environment is equally important for fostering openness and receptiveness among the participants. Everyone should feel at ease, both physically and emotionally. Arrange seating in a circle to encourage camaraderie and connection. Soft cushions or blankets can help make the space inviting, and having elements like ambient music or nature sounds in the background can enhance the experience further.

During my events, I noticed that incorporating elements like gentle lighting—perhaps with fairy lights or candles—adds to a sense of wonder while also reducing the harshness of typical illumination. Besides physical comfort, emotional safety is paramount. It helps to start with an icebreaker or a meditation session where everyone shares their intentions for the evening. This helps participants to connect on a personal level, creating a joint energy for the forthcoming summoning. Remember, when individuals feel comfortable and valued, the energy they collectively generate can be incredibly powerful.

One practical tip to keep in mind is to encourage participants to bring personal items that hold meaning to them, such as crystals or photographs. Not only does this foster personal investment in the event, but it also invites different energies into the gathering. Each object can serve as a unique focal point, sparking conversations and connections that deepen the collective experience. The power of summoning UFOs lies not just in the physical act but also in the emotional and spiritual bonds we create during these gatherings.

12.3 Communal Energy Dynamics and Their Effects

Group dynamics are often overlooked in the context of summoning, yet they can significantly influence the energy flow. When individuals gather with a shared purpose, a unique energy forms, transcending the individual contributions of each person. During our own summoning sessions, I've felt this energy shift palpably. It's as though the collective intention amplifies our thoughts and feelings, creating a resonance that aligns with what we seek to invite into our experience. This phenomenon isn't just theoretical; I've seen it in action. One evening, as we convened under a starry sky, our individual hopes and dreams melded into a singular vibration, and I could almost hear it humming in the air. It seems that when we gather with open hearts and focused minds, we create a conduit for something larger and more powerful than ourselves.

Many summoning groups report a range of collective experiences that highlight this communal energy. After sharing our thoughts and intentions aloud, participants often describe sensations of warmth, tingling, or an undeniable connection to the environment around us. In one particular session, we focused on a designated time for the appearance of a UFO. As we chanted and visualized, several members claimed to see flickers of light in the sky before the stillness of the night enveloped us. Others felt an overwhelming sense of peace, as if the universe had whispered back to us in response to our unified call. These moments are not just coincidences; they are evidence of our communal energy in action. It's fascinating to witness how shared willingness can elevate our experiences, nurturing bonds not just with one another, but with the cosmos.

As we delve deeper into understanding these dynamics, one practical tip stands out: establish a pre-summoning ritual that reinforces your group's connection. Taking a few moments to ground yourselves, perhaps through meditation or shared breathing exercises, can enhance your collective energy. This practice can draw each participant into the same energetic sphere, thereby amplifying the intent behind your summoning efforts. The more attuned you become to each other's energy, the greater the potential for remarkable experiences during your gatherings. Remember, it's not just about the destination or the sighting; it's about the journey and the energy you cultivate together as a community.

Chapter 13: Navigating the Aftermath of UFO Encounters

13.1 Processing Emotional and Spiritual Aftereffects

Experiencing a UFO encounter can stir a whirlwind of emotions. It's not just the awe of seeing something unexplained; it can also bring feelings of confusion, fear, or even isolation. Many people who have had such experiences describe a sense of exhilaration that is often accompanied by an equally powerful dose of anxiety. You might find yourself questioning the nature of reality, grappling with feelings of not being understood by those around you. These emotional impacts can linger long after the encounter is over, creating a tumultuous space within. I recall my own experience where I felt an overwhelming sense of connection to something vast and indescribable, but also a creeping doubt about whether anyone would believe me or how I could share these feelings. It's essential to recognize these raw emotions and gently process them rather than suppressing or dismissing them.

Healing from a UFO encounter involves acknowledging what you felt and giving yourself the space to explore those feelings without judgment. One effective strategy is journaling, writing down not just the details of the encounter, but also your emotions surrounding it. This practice can help untangle those confusing feelings. Meditation can also be a powerful tool, allowing you to sit with your thoughts and feelings in a calm environment. I have found that visualizing a safe, comforting place during meditation can help channel the intense emotions into a more serene state. Connecting with others who have had similar experiences, whether through online forums or meet-up groups, can also provide a sense of belonging and validation. Sharing your story might help in releasing some of that weight. It's important to remember that you are not alone in feeling this way.

Practicing self-care is fundamental, especially after such profound experiences. This could range from physical activities like jogging or yoga to creative outlets like painting or music. All of these help to channel energy positively. Grounding exercises can be particularly useful; they involve connecting with the earth to regain a sense of stability. Techniques such as deep breathing or focusing on your senses—what you can see, smell, feel, and hear—can bring you back to the present moment and provide a sense of calm. And finally, always remember to trust your intuition. If a certain practice or community feels right for you, dive into it. It can guide you on your path to emotional and spiritual healing.

13.2 Reporting and Sharing Findings

Sharing our personal encounters with the unknown can create a sense of community and inspire others to explore their own experiences. I remember the first time I saw what I believed to be a UFO; it was exhilarating, and I felt compelled to document every detail. Capturing the date, time, location, and even the emotions I felt made the experience more vivid and impactful. This practice of documentation is crucial because it ensures that our experiences are recorded accurately, and it gives us a chance to reflect on them later. I encourage everyone to keep a dedicated notebook or digital diary where you can jot down your sightings, feelings, and the circumstances surrounding them. Consider including sketches or photos if you have them. When we share these rich narratives with others—whether in online forums, social media groups, or at local meetups—we not only validate our journeys but also open the door for others to feel inspired and empowered to share their stories as well.

Reporting findings goes beyond individual experiences; it is about creating a tapestry of knowledge that helps us all understand these mysteries a bit better. When I started sharing my findings, I didn't realize how crucial my voice and perspective would be. Each report, whether it be a photograph, a detailed account, or even a simple observation, plays a role in shaping our collective understanding of unidentified flying objects. By compiling and sharing our documented experiences, we form a mosaic of sightings and encounters that can provide insights into patterns or behaviors of these phenomena. This sharing creates a ripple effect; one person's sighting might resonate with someone else's experience, prompting new investigations or inquiries. We inspire curiosity and engagement. So, when you come across interesting data or have a breakthrough moment, take the time to write it down and share it. You never know who else might be searching for answers—and your findings could guide them.

Consider joining a local UFO group or an online community to disseminate your insights and learn from others. Engaging in discussions about your findings not only nurtures your own understanding but also enriches the collective learning experience for everyone involved.

13.3 Integrating Experiences into Daily Life

Incorporating insights gained from UFO encounters into daily practice requires an open mind and a willingness to explore the unknown. Every time I have had an encounter, whether it was a fleeting glimpse of a strange light in the sky or a more intense experience, there were lessons woven into those moments. I learned to embrace curiosity and to pay closer attention to the world around me. I began to prioritize moments of stillness and reflection, allowing myself the space to connect with these insights. The key is to keep a journal, not just to document sightings but also to capture the emotions and thoughts that arise post-experience. This can lead to personal insights that may guide your daily decisions and actions, creating a continuous cycle of learning and growth. It is essential to integrate practices such as meditation or mindfulness that can help in grounding these experiences into my practical life. When I meditate, I often visualize the moments I've had, revisiting those feelings of wonder and connection to the cosmos. This practice helps solidify the insights I've gathered, merging them with my present reality.

The connectivity of these experiences to personal growth unfolds naturally as I reflect upon them. Each encounter stirs a deep sense of connection, not only to the universe but to my inner self and to those around me. It prompts me to ask important questions about existence, purpose, and the role we play in the vast tapestry of life. As I share my experiences with like-minded individuals, I find that these stories foster community and understanding, enriching both my world and theirs. The integration of insights transforms not only how I see myself but also how I interact with the people in my life. I notice a greater kindness in my actions and an increased willingness to engage in conversations about the unexplainable. Embracing the mystery of UFO encounters has helped me leave behind limiting beliefs and has amplified my appreciation for the subtleties of life. One practical way to enhance your personal growth through these experiences is to connect with a community or online forum where enthusiasts share their stories and perspectives. This exchange can provide new insights and encourage deeper reflection on your own experiences.

As you explore these themes and work to encompass them in your life, remember that every step of the journey counts. Let your curiosity lead you; dedicate some time each week to ponder these experiences and how they shape your reality. Not only can you summon UFOs into your life, but you can also invite growth, understanding, and an ongoing conversation with the universe. Embrace the mystery, integrate it with intention, and allow it to inspire you each day.

Chapter 14: Ethical Considerations in UFO Summoning

14.1 Respecting the Space of Extraterrestrial Beings

When it comes to summoning extraterrestrial beings, understanding the importance of consent and respect is paramount. The very act of reaching out to entities from beyond our world requires that we acknowledge their autonomy and right to choose. This isn't merely about asking them to come; it's about inviting them into a space that respects their existence as sentient beings. I've come to realize that every time I prepare for a summoning session, I make it a point to call upon them with a tone of genuine respect. I softly express my intentions and desires, making it clear that I am honored to be in their presence should they decide to join me. This respectful approach, I believe, creates a more harmonious environment that may encourage a response, rather than imposing my will upon them. A ritual of gratitude, including offerings of kindness or even simple words of thanks, can set the right tone for this interaction, reminding both myself and the otherworldly entities of the mutual respect that ought to exist.

Engaging with extraterrestrial beings also leads us to consider the ethical guidelines that should guide our interactions. It's easy to overlook the fact that these entities might have their own customs, desires, and boundaries which need to be acknowledged. The dialogues with these beings must be rooted in mutual respect and understanding. During one of my encounters, I felt an overwhelming sensation that signaled it was time to step back. Recognizing this cue taught me the importance of allowing space; it is not only respectful but essential for a meaningful interaction. Establishing an open line of communication is crucial, but one must ensure that it is a two-way street. Inviting them to share their thoughts, experiences, or even concerns creates a deeper connection and reinforces that we are equals in this exchange, rather than mere observers or exploiters.

As I reflect on my experiences, I can't help but emphasize the significance of maintaining a humble heart. When engaging with beings from other dimensions, one should remain open and receptive. Every encounter is not just about gathering information or documenting experiences. It's about creating a dialogue where both parties can learn and grow. Maintaining that mindset turns what could be a simple summoning into a rich, transformative experience. A practical tip would be to keep a journal of your thoughts and feelings after each session, giving you a space to process the experiences and insights from your interactions. It reinforces the lesson that while we reach out into the cosmos, we must also respect and honor whatever follows.

14.2 Establishing Boundaries in Your Practices

Establishing personal boundaries is crucial when embarking on summoning activities. These boundaries create a safe space where I can explore my intentions without external interference. I learned early on that the energy I project can significantly influence my experiences, especially when it comes to connecting with UFOs. By clearly defining what I am comfortable with, I can enhance my focus and increase the likelihood of a successful encounter. It's essential to spend some quiet time reflecting on what these boundaries look like for me, whether it's designating specific times for summoning, selecting safe locations, or even determining the level of openness I wish to maintain with others about my experiences.

I've found that setting a time and place for my sessions helps me mentally prepare and align my thoughts. This ritualistic approach gives me a sense of control and ownership over the process. Not only does it foster a deeper connection to my intentions, but it also signals to the universe that I'm serious about my practice. When I'm grounded in my boundaries, I'm less likely to be swayed by doubts or external noise from those who might not share my beliefs. It's about creating that sanctity around the act of summoning, allowing it to be a personal and profound experience.

When I started implementing strong personal boundaries into my summoning practices, I noticed a marked improvement in my experiences. By creating a defined space, it's as though I crafted a conduit between my energy and that of the universe. This separation clears away distractions and allows me to enter a state of heightened awareness. Without boundaries, it's too easy to be overrun by fears or suggestions from others, which can muddle my intentions and the energies I wish to attract.

To cultivate a successful summoning environment, it's practical to write down my boundaries, keep them in a safe space, and revisit them regularly. This reminder keeps me anchored and focused, ensuring that as I progress in my practices, I maintain a sense of personal integrity and safety.

14.3 Maintaining a Balanced Exchange of Energy

Energy reciprocity is crucial when it comes to summoning practices, especially for those of us engaging with otherworldly beings. I've learned through my experiences that these unseen forces are highly sensitive to the energies we emit. When you're inviting UFOs or other entities into your space, what you put out is often what you attract. If we approach these summoning sessions with an imbalance of energy—whether it's too much excitement, fear, or a lack of intention—the results can be unpredictable or even disappointing. A harmonious flow of energy paves the way for clear communication. Think of it like a dance: the energy between you and what you're trying to summon must be synchronized; otherwise, you might end up stepping on each other's toes, so to speak.

One strategy I found effective for ensuring balanced energy exchange involves grounding yourself before beginning any summoning practice. Find a quiet space where you can connect with the Earth. Visualize roots extending from your body into the ground, absorbing stability and strength. This allows you to anchor your energy and maintain a calm state, which is essential when you're attempting to connect with higher frequencies. Additionally, utilizing crystals that promote energy balance can help create a protective barrier around your space, allowing for a more suitable environment for these interactions. Before you commence your session, take a moment to set your intention and send gratitude into the universe. Expressing appreciation not only enhances your vibrational frequency but also opens a channel for reciprocity, as beings from other realms often respond kindly to sincere energy exchanges.

Another practical tip is to experiment with the timing of your sessions. I have found that early mornings or late nights can hold unique energy qualities ideal for summoning. The quietude of these hours often allows for deeper concentration and resonance with the energies you wish to invoke. Pay attention to how your body feels in these different conditions and adjust your practices accordingly. Maintaining this balance is an ongoing journey—it's about tuning into your energy and the energy around you, continually cultivating an atmosphere of respect and harmony with the entities you wish to connect with.

Chapter 15: Expanding Your Knowledge and Community

15.1 Resources for Continued Learning

To dive deeper into the fascinating world of UFO summoning, there are a variety of excellent resources that can expand your understanding. Books such as The Complete Guide to Alien Encounters provide insights into different methods and experiences from others who have attempted to connect with extraterrestrial beings. Many articles available online explore personal testimonies and detailed accounts from individuals who claim to have successfully summoned UFOs, offering practical tips and guidance. Engaging with community forums and blogs dedicated to this subject can also reveal a plethora of shared knowledge, where enthusiasts exchange strategies and stories. Websites like the Mutual UFO Network (MUFON) and the Center for the Study of Extraterrestrial Intelligence (CSETI) feature valuable articles and research papers that discuss the scientific and spiritual aspects of UFO phenomena, providing a well-rounded view of the subject. Documentaries and podcasts are also fantastic mediums; they often present interviews with experts that shed light on the multifaceted nature of UFO encounters and how they relate to summoning practices.

Ongoing education in the field of UFO summoning is essential for anyone serious about making meaningful connections with the unknown. I encourage you to participate in workshops and local meetups that focus on UFO awareness and summoning techniques. These gatherings often expose you to new ideas and alternative approaches to connecting with UFOs, fostering a sense of community and support. Engaging with experienced practitioners can provide mentorship opportunities and firsthand accounts that are invaluable to your growth. Explore courses on meditation and consciousness expansion, as these practices can enhance your ability to open up to extraterrestrial energies. Remember, the pursuit of knowledge in this field is ongoing, and every experience can teach you something new. Approaching your learning with curiosity and openness will not only enrich your understanding but also elevate your practice, bringing you closer to the experiences you seek.

Keep a journal of your experiences and insights as you progress on this journey. Reflecting on your thoughts and feelings after each attempt can illuminate patterns or responses you might not notice in the moment, allowing you to fine-tune your techniques. This reflective practice can transform every encounter into a valuable lesson, paving the way for successful UFO summoning.

15.2 Building Networks with Like-Minded Individuals

Finding a community that shares your interests can be incredibly rewarding, especially when it comes to something as fascinating and enigmatic as UFO summoning. The journey to connect with the universe is often less solitary when accompanied by others who are equally curious and eager to learn. Being part of a supportive community provides not only encouragement but also a wealth of knowledge and shared experiences. When we gather with others who have a similar passion, we create an environment where ideas can flow freely, questions can be asked without judgment, and discoveries can be celebrated together. This sense of belonging brings a level of motivation that is hard to achieve alone. The more we exchange thoughts and techniques, the deeper our understanding becomes. No matter where you are in your journey, surrounding yourself with those who fuel your passion can open new doors and push the boundaries of what you might have thought possible.

Connecting with others interested in UFO summoning takes some initiative, but the rewards are well worth the effort. Start by searching online forums dedicated to UFO phenomena or joining social media groups where members share their experiences and tips. Websites like Reddit have vibrant communities where you can engage in discussions or ask questions. Attend local meetups or workshops focused on UFO studies; not only will you meet individuals who are as passionate as you, but you may also stumble upon mentors who can guide you down your path. Engaging in conversations at these events can lead to lasting friendships, while also giving you diverse perspectives that challenge and expand your own understanding. Additionally, consider starting your own group if there isn't one nearby. Hosting open invitation nights where enthusiasts can gather to share stories and practices can help cultivate a sense of community in your area.

Remember, building these networks takes time and effort, but making the investment is crucial for your personal growth in UFO summoning. The more you connect and engage with others, the more resources and experiences you will have at your disposal. This journey is not just about reaching for the stars; it's about fostering connections that help pave the way to those distant worlds. Keep an open mind, be respectful of others' experiences, and never hesitate to share what you know. You may be surprised at how much you can learn from just one conversation. Finally, consider keeping a journal of your experiences and meetings—this record will not only help you track your progress but can also serve as a conversation starter when connecting with new friends.

15.3 Engaging with Workshops and Conferences

Engaging with workshops and conferences can open a world of opportunities for anyone interested in learning how to summon UFOs. These events often gather enthusiasts, researchers, and professionals who share a mutual curiosity about the unknown. By attending these educational gatherings, you not only gain access to cutting-edge research but also connect with individuals who share your passion. Many workshops offer hands-on activities, where you can practice techniques for increased connection with the cosmos. The conversations and networking that happen at these conferences can ignite your creativity, offering insights that you might not find in books or online forums. The experiential aspect of workshops deepens your understanding, as you engage directly with speakers and participants who have firsthand experiences or empirical knowledge on the subject.

I remember attending a fascinating conference on UFOs in a small town known for its rich history of sightings. The atmosphere buzzed with the excitement of people eager to share their stories. A panel discussion featured a well-known researcher who had spent years investigating UFO phenomena. Listening to him describe his firsthand encounters was captivating and surreal. After the talk, I approached him and found myself deep in conversation about my own experiences and theories. It was thrilling to bounce ideas around in real time, and it felt incredibly validating to speak with someone who understood my perspective. The connections I made during that conference led me to collaborative projects, and some friendships have lasted years.

Furthermore, the workshops I attended often focused on practical skills—such as meditation techniques to enhance intuition or methods for creating a conducive environment for sightings. Learning in a collaborative setting added depth and fun to the experience; being surrounded by like-minded individuals heightened my motivation. These gatherings aren't just about absorbing knowledge; they're also about building a community of adventure seekers who chase the unexplained. As you seek out workshops and conferences, remember to be open to new ideas and personal stories, as they can enrich your journey immensely. One practical tip is to engage with the community both during and after the event—whether through social media or local meetups—to continue the discussions and keep the momentum alive.

Also by Jessie Contreras

Messages from the Stars: A Guide to Summoning the Galactic Federation
Celestial Awakening: Ascension and the Art of Summoning UFOs
Energy Vortexes: Harnessing Power for UFO Summoning
The Alien Code: Unlocking the Matrix
The Ultimate UFO Summoning Guide:2026 Edition
How To Master The Ancient Art Of Summoning Motherships
The Resonant Universe: Bioelectrical Energy And The Call Of UFOs
UFOs and the Art of Mimicry: The Hidden Intelligence Behind the Disguise

About the Author

Jessie Contreras is a dedicated researcher of unidentified aerial phenomena whose work blends disciplined observation with an interest in how human consciousness shapes extraordinary experiences. Guided by a lifelong fascination with the night sky, he shares his insights through community work, educational content, and continued study. His mission is to explore the phenomenon with clarity, integrity, and an unwavering commitment to understanding what lies beyond the familiar.

About the Publisher

Summon UFOs is a forward-thinking publishing brand dedicated to exploring the intersection of consciousness, extraterrestrial contact, and human potential. Through its works, the brand presents innovative perspectives on UFO phenomena, blending experiential practices, emerging technologies, and esoteric knowledge into a cohesive framework for understanding and initiating contact. Summon UFOs aims to inspire curiosity, expand awareness, and empower individuals to engage with the unknown in a structured, intentional, and transformative way.